**SCHIRMER PERFORMANCE EDITIONS**

# PROKOFIEV

## VISIONS FUGITIVES

Opus 22

LABORUM DULCE LENIMEN

G. SCHIRMER

Edited and Recorded by Alexandre Dossin

To access companion recorded performances online, visit:
**www.halleonard.com/mylibrary**

Enter Code
6852-5198-1471-8676

On the cover:
*In Blue* (1925)
by Wassily Kandinsky
(1866–1944)

ISBN 978-1-4234-9413-3

# G. SCHIRMER, Inc.

DISTRIBUTED BY

HAL•LEONARD®
CORPORATION

7777 W. BLUEMOUND RD. P.O. BOX 13819 MILWAUKEE, WI 53213

Copyright © 2011 by G. Schirmer, Inc. (ASCAP) New York, NY
International Copyright Secured. All Rights Reserved.

Warning: Unauthorized reproduction of this publication is
prohibited by Federal law and subject to criminal prosecution.

www.schirmer.com
**www.halleonard.com**

# CONTENTS

The price of this publication includes access to companion recorded performances online, for download or streaming, using the unique code found on the title page. Visit **www.halleonard.com/mylibrary** and enter the access code.

# HISTORICAL NOTES

## SERGEI PROKOFIEV (1891–1953)

The late 19th century was a rather tumultuous time in music history, as many opposing thoughts and opinions on music itself were at great odds with each other. The essential principles of Romanticism were still prominent, as evidenced by Tchaikovsky and Mahler, yet modernism was on the horizon, as seen in the works of Schoenberg, Ives, and Stravinsky. While many embraced the "new" sound, many musicians, composers, and listeners were openly critical of it. Into this clash of styles and philosophies, Sergei Prokofiev was born in 1891 in the Russian city of Sontsovka.

His mother, Maria Grigoryevna Zhitkova, guided his earliest lessons. She was a pianist of some skill, and would often play the family piano for hours as the young Sergei listened. At the age of four, he began to experiment on the piano himself, and in his autobiography, he recalls this description of his early creativity:

"On the one hand, I would work out little motifs that I was as yet unable to jot down. On the other hand, while sitting at the piano I would jot down notes that meant nothing. I drew them as ornaments, the way children draw people and trains, simply because I had always seen music on the piano."[1]

Eventually, he did create his first "real" tune, and his mother notated it for him. The resulting work, "Indian Galop," was written when he was 5 years old. (See the musical sample at the bottom of this page.)

He later commented that "...the lack of a B-flat should not be attributed to a sympathy for the Lydian mode. Rather, the inexperienced composer had not yet decided to touch the black keys."[2] From that point forward, Prokofiev's life would be consumed with composition, completing symphonies and operas before he was a teenager. While these works are generally not considered much more than untrained attempts at composing, many of them contain moments that are clear previews of the Prokofiev sound we now recognize in his mature works.

Prokofiev continued to mature at the St. Petersburg Conservatory, which he entered in 1904 to study piano and composition. Often the youngest in his composition class by as many as eight years, he studied with some of the greatest names in Russian music, including Rimsky-Korsakov and Lyadov. He was frequently chided by his professors for the unconventional elements of his music, yet he picked his battles carefully, appeasing in one situation, and deliberately provoking in another. His independence and exploration of new ideas, combined with a healthy respect for the traditions of the past, joined together to produce his singular style as a composer.

During and after his time at the Conservatory, Prokofiev found growing success as a performer, and as a composer. Many of his early works were premiered with great praise on a concert series in St. Petersburg called "Evenings of Contemporary Music." He worked with Diaghilev on several ballets, and completed the first two piano concertos. His music never caused a riot on the scale of that which occurred at the premiere of Stravinsky's *Rite of Spring*, yet he did receive plenty of criticism from the more conservative elements in Russia.

In 1918, shortly after the Bolshevik Revolution, and with the permission of the Russian Cultural Commissar, Prokofiev left his homeland to tour the world. During this long period of travel—he did not return to Russia until 1936—Prokofiev lived and performed in the United States and Europe. His compositions from this period include the famous third Piano Concerto, and his most successful opera, *The Love for Three Oranges*.

As early as 1932, he began to consider returning permanently to Russia, which had undergone significant political changes since his departure. Music was more closely scrutinized in this new government, and composers' works were subject to review and revision. In his personal diaries, Prokofiev expressed private concern about the political climate, but felt that he might find new opportunities musically there.[3] In 1936, he returned permanently.

Film-scoring became one of his "new opportunities," and in Russia he wrote the score for several patriotic films, including the famous *Alexander Nevsky*. Yet his penchant for the new and unique could not be completely suppressed, and gradually he began to come under criticism and stern governmental oversight. In 1949, several of his works were officially banned from being programmed on any concerts in Russia. In spite of these challenging conditions he composed many significant works in the 1940s, including his most famous symphony, Symphony No. 5.

He died in 1953, ironically on the same day as his oppressor Stalin. As a result, far less attention was given to his passing than might have been otherwise. Yet he left behind a large and important body of work, in a wide variety of genres, and is considered one of the greatest of the 20th century composers.

—*Matthew Edwards*
Editor of *Prokofiev: Music for Children*, Op. 65

# PERFORMANCE NOTES

## Introduction to Prokofiev's Piano Music

The piano played a very important role in Prokofiev's development as a musician. His technique was considered idiosyncratic, and he always managed to impress his audiences with his steel rhythm and emotional performances, without using external, theatrical effects.

Prokofiev's piano music is vast and consists of a wide diversity of works, from simple and short miniatures, to the great group of nine piano sonatas. It certainly could be argued that the piano sonatas alone would be enough to guarantee Prokofiev's name in the gallery of great piano composers. In addition to this impressive series of works, there are wonderful sets of smaller pieces including etudes, preludes, gavottes, minuets, and toccatas; and larger works with unique titles such as *Tales of an Old Grandmother*, *Visions Fugitives*, *Things in Themselves*, *Sarcasms*, and others.

His piano style incorporates toccata-style, lyricism, classical clarity, modern techniques, and satiric/sarcastic elements. The level of technical expertise required to perform his music ranges from the early intermediate *Music for the Young* to the highly advanced sonatas, Toccata, Op. 11, and many more.

### Fingering

Fingerings are editorial and have in mind a medium-sized hand. Some adjustments may be needed for smaller hands. As a rule, fingerings were carefully chosen to convey the phrasing and articulation, not simply for comfort. Two numbers connected by a hyphen represent a slide between black and white keys; two numbers connected by a slur represent a finger substitution. In some cases, an optional fingering is shown under or above in parenthesis.

### Pedaling

It is practically impossible to notate pedaling in an effective way. Good pedaling depends on many variables (quality of the instrument, performer's touch, how far the pedal is depressed, specific acoustics, etc.), that any effort becomes almost pointless, since the performer will need to make the final decisions, using his or her musical abilities and sensibilities. Therefore, pedal indications are only suggestions, needing fine tuning for the specific performer, instrument, and concert hall. In the sections where effective pedaling is almost impossible to notate or too obvious, it is omitted altogether. Except for instances where a special sound effect is needed, good pedaling is not supposed to be heard. In other words, use the pedal in such a way so that the textures are always clear and not compromised by excessive blurring. The indication *no ped.* means: use as little pedal as possible, usually in very light, staccato textures.

### Metronome markings

Metronome markings are editorial. Instead of suggesting a specific marking, a small range of possible tempos is provided. In the editor's opinion, performances outside those markings may lack the necessary clarity if too fast, or may not allow for correct phrasing if too slow.

### Dynamics and Articulation

Dynamics and articulation are Prokofiev's throughout.

## Visions Fugitives, Op. 22

The title of this collection of twenty miniatures was inspired by a poem by Konstantin Balmont:

> In every fleeting vision I see worlds
> Filled with the fickle play of rainbows

The Russian word "mimolyotnosti" translates loosely as "fleeting vision," and the French title "Visions Fugitives" was suggested to Prokofiev by Balmont's wife (Prokofiev Diaries, 1915–1923, p. 221).

Most elements of Prokofiev's pianistic style are present in this elegant set. One could argue that composers feel freer to experiment when working on small pieces. Studying such works could be compared to witnessing the composer's creative laboratory of ideas coming alive.

The twenty short pieces with timing ranging from just under thirty seconds to a little more than two minutes were not composed in the order they were published, nor in the same period of time. Prokofiev wrote the pieces between 1915 and 1917. He decided the final order not based on chronology, but on musical content. Thus the set starts and ends with slow pieces, with fast and rhythmic movements interspersed. It was performed for the first time by Prokofiev as a set in Kislovodsk, on October 14, 1917. On the same concert, the third sonata had its premiere. Prokofiev referred to that evening in his diary: "... the audience may not have particularly enjoyed what I played, but I did enjoy the way I played it" (Prokofiev Diaries, 1915–1923, p. 235).

Each year impressed different emotions on the individual works: the 1915 pieces (5, 6, 10, 16 and 17) tend to be in a light and positive mood, while the majority of 1917 selections (1, 4, 8, 9, 11, 14, 15, 18, and 19) reflect the changing political winds in revolutionary Russia. In general, a more pensive mood is reflected in the 1916 compositions (2, 3, 7, 12, 13, and 20). Some of the tempo indications are very creative and include uncommon expressions such as *"ridiculosamente,"* *"molto giocoso,"* *"con eleganza,"* *"pittoresco,"* *"feroce,"* *"inquieto,"* *"poetico,"* *"lento irrealmente,"* and *"con una dolce lentezza."*

Several transcriptions and orchestrations of the set as well as individual movements have been made; in addition, Prokofiev mentioned that Adolph Bolm danced to the set in the Brooklyn Museum, in 1918 (Prokofiev Diaries, 1915–1923, p. 348). There are several recordings of the entire cycle and recordings that include only selections. From those recordings, the editor would like to call attention to two live recordings by Arthur Rubinstein (12 pieces), a Sviatoslav Richter's performance of three pieces, and Emil Gilels' recording of 8 pieces. Gould's performance of number 2 is very different from all other performances, with an incredibly slow tempo (quarter note = c. 38) giving the piece an eerie characteristic, not usually heard on performances that follow the *andante*

tempo marking. Prokofiev recorded nine of the pieces in 1935 (nos. 9, 3, 17, 18, 11, 10, 16, 6, and 5). His performances will be briefly described under each piece's commentary. Even though performing the set as a whole is a very pleasant experience, excerpts may be chosen, in any order. It is interesting to note that often recordings of excerpts (including Prokofiev's own recording) do not follow the published order.

# Performance Notes on the Individual Pieces

### 1. Lentamente

The contemplative opening piece varies two statements of the same idea (mm. 1–8 and 14–21) with *misterioso* sections interpolated (mm. 9–13 and 22–27). Dynamic markings are in the soft range from *ppp* to *mp*. The keyword is simplicity: Prokofiev requests the first section to be performed *"con una semplicità espressiva"* and the second statement *"semplice."* Perform this piece in long phrases and use overlapping pedal for better legato.

### 2. Andante

This slightly "jazzy" miniature requires a deliberate choice of tempo, so as notes are added in the right hand (mm. 7–10), the overall pulse remains the same. On the fourth beat of mm. 14 and 15, one needs to push the keys down (D in m. 14 and the open fifth G–D in m. 15) without allowing the hammer to strike the strings, for a nice pedaling to be achieved. As in the first piece, Prokofiev asks for a *misterioso* quality in the answer to the main idea. Depending on the piano, the left pedal may be used to explore that sonority.

### 3. Allegretto

The writing here has several textures, and should be noticed by the performer. Avoid too much pedal, connecting the right-hand chords with finger legato and allowing the left hand to display the two-part texture. Important contrast should be explored in mm. 13–22, with good textural differentiation—staccatos and accents in the right hand versus a two-part pedal point in the left hand. Prokofiev mentions in his diaries that a young lady asked him after a performance of this piece what was the key of it, and he could not answer, adding in parenthesis: "tonalities are not something I ever think about" (Prokofiev Diaries, 1915–1923, p. 431). On his recording, Prokofiev chooses a moderate tempo in the A section (quarter = 126) and speeds up a little in the middle section. His approach is subdued, without big contrasts.

### 4. Animato

This piece, composed in 1917, displays a harsh, violent character. A strong technique is required in order to perform this work in a fast and decisive tempo. The *più sostenuto* section (from m. 29 to the end) should be played without pedal, very staccato. Thinking in terms of orchestra: allow the legato bassoon melody to come alive within the *pizzicato* texture.

### 5. Molto giocoso

The shortest of the cycle, this piece lasts less than 30 seconds. It was inspired by a wedding of Prokofiev's close friends. From m. 8 to the end, the piece is played with pedal, not lifting until the end. This creates the effect of tolling bells. The playful character should be explored in the first eight measures, exaggerating the articulation markings. Prokofiev starts his performance with a fast-paced, quarter = 152 tempo. In m. 8 there is a noticeable change of tempo, slowing down to quarter = 108.

### 6. Con eleganza

Another very brief piece in ABA form; the second A section repeats the main section completely until the very end, where the last chord is altered (compare mm. 8 and 24). The B section has a left-hand pedal point accompanying the right hand's upward-soaring melody. No pedal is necessary in this piece, and great care should be taken to follow Prokofiev's "breathing" indications (eight-note rests). The sign above the right hand in measures 2 and 18 indicate a lift or small (very small) pause. Some recordings exaggerate this effect. In Prokofiev's performance, the sign simply makes the previous note staccato, without any rest or change in tempo. On his recording, Prokofiev chose a very brisk tempo for this piece: dotted quarter note = 168, with the eight-notes sounding almost like grace notes.

### 7. Pittoresco (Harp)

This is the only piece with a title. The harp quality should be explored through a careful use of pedal, including half-pedals. The main melody starts in m. 7 after six introductory, mood-creating measures. The accented Fs (second beat of mm. 8, 18, and 26) are not part of the melody and should be played with the second finger, differentiating it from the overall texture.

### 8. Comodo

This polyphonic work requires great care in the choice of touch. The touch should allow the main melody (mm. 1–4) to be always recognized, especially as the textures grow more complex. The choice of tempo is also important: too slow and it will drag, too fast and it will be agitated, instead of the required comfortable. As with many of the works in the set, this one explores the contrast between sharp keys and Prokofiev's beloved all-white keys. The change in color from m. 4 to 5 should be explored.

### 9. Allegretto tranquillo

This is a charming piece that creates a *"perpetuum mobile"* effect through its constant motion in eighth-notes and sixteenth-notes. Pedal can be used, especially if great care is taken to keep the touch light and fleeting. The long whole notes in the bass (mm. 8–9 and 20–23) should be held with pedal. Pianists with small hands will have problem performing this piece due to the parallel tenths that are required (mm. 1–2, 16–19, 29–30). Breaking the tenths weakens their effect, and should be avoided if possible. Prokofiev's performance tempo varies from quarter = 104 to quarter = 126. His use of *rubato* is very noticeable, and the overall texture becomes almost impressionistic at times.

### 10. Ridiculosamente

Probably one of the most famous and most often recorded from the set, this piece explores Prokofiev's sarcastic style: a staccato bassoon line contrasts with obsessive Fs in the right hand. Sometimes the Fs go up an octave, sometimes up a sixth (mm. 3–10), until they start an angular melodic fragment, only to be cut by descending 5-finger position little runs (mm. 15–17). Because this piece is so often recorded, the choice of tempos vary greatly from around 70 to over 120 for the quarter note. Prokofiev's recording has a metronome marking of around 96 for the quarter note, and he uses quite a lot of *rubato* in his performance. In m. 24, last eighth-note in the left hand, some editions have G-flat–B-flat instead of F–A. Prokofiev plays F–A

### 11. Con vivacità

Once more, articulation is key for a proper performance of this piece. The left hand keeps an almost *ostinato pizzicato* texture in the A section, contrasting with the right hand's short, accented motives. Overall dynamics should be soft and the touch very light. The middle section requires a nice legato, with light staccato quarter notes. A performance tradition (possibly started by Prokofiev) suggests this section to be a little slower. Prokofiev's tempo is a brisk 184 for the quarter note in the A section, contrasted by a moderate 126 in the middle section. However, his rhythmic command is such that the change is barely noticeable in the performance.

### 12. Assai moderato

This slow waltz should be performed with a sense of dance, keeping the pulse steady, always observing Prokofiev's use of slurs versus rests. Don't allow pedaling to cover those details.

### 13. Allegretto

A great study in trills, this piece requires good polyphonic control, especially in the right hand. Dynamic range is from *pp* to *p*, helping to create a subdued overall feeling. Keeping the pulse in a slow two instead of a faster four will help to find an appropriate tempo.

### 14. Feroce

*Feroce* is not used very often as a tempo marking description. However, it fits this very aggressive, obsessive miniature composed in 1917 when Russia was experiencing revolutionary times. A firm but flexible wrist will be needed for a rhythmic and strong performance. This piece has a violent *ostinato* feel, making it an unnerving ride, despite its short duration. A fast, decisive tempo is paramount without any *rubato* or *ritardando*.

### 15. Inquieto

The tempo marking, coupled with the indications "*pp una corda e senza ped.*" give the full picture of this nervous, unsettled piece. A good fingering is important to avoid the use of pedal, while at the same time allowing a smooth performance. This is not a staccato piece. In mm. 10–11, there is a discrepancy in the scores consulted: some editions add a sharp to the left-hand C on the fourth beat of m. 10, keeping it sharp all the way through m. 11. Other editions add the sharp only to the second beat, left-hand C of m. 11. There is no consensus on the recordings consulted.

### 16. Dolente

The contrast between the A and B parts should be explored not only through dynamics, but principally through a change of touch: heavy and thick in the first section, light and soft in the middle section (not playful, though—this is a sad, *dolente* piece). Prokofiev's tempo in this piece is on the fast side (quarter = 112, with a slightly slower tempo in the middle section), using a very elegant *rubato*.

### 17. Poetico

The softest piece in the cycle, this is performed by Prokofiev in an almost impressionistic style. With dynamic markings of *ppp* to *pp*, be very careful with the touch and choice of tempo. Both pedals can be used, and fluttering the right pedal gives the mysterious, eerie feel that this work requires. No variation in the tempo, nor *ritardando* at the end is needed. Prokofiev's tempo is quite fast (quarter = 168); he uses a very soft touch throughout.

### 18.  Con una dolce lentezza

This is another gentle waltz, but with a tender feel. The left-hand rhythmic *ostinato* figure (half-note, quarter-note) allows for a subtle *rubato* to be used, as long as Prokofiev's indicated phrasing is correctly followed. I suggest half-pedal changes for mm. 30 and 31, in order for the B of m. 29 to remain ringing to the end.  Prokofiev's tempo is around 88 for the quarter-note, with exquisite use of *rubato* and a very gentle performance.

### 19. Presto agitatissimo e molto accentuato

This piece was composed around the February, 1917 revolution in Russia. Prokofiev refers to it in his autobiography: "The 19th Vision Fugitive, written around this time [February, 1917], in part reflects impressions—more the agitation of the crowd than the inner essence of the Revolution" (Short Autobiography, cited in Prokofiev Diaries, 1915–1923, p. 184n.).

It is the most aggressive and technically challenging of the cycle. A fast and unrelenting tempo is required throughout. I suggest the fingering change in mm. 38–39 for a stronger ending.

### 20. Lento irrealmente

It is interesting to note that Prokofiev chose this particular piece to end the cycle. It was composed in 1916, and does not have the typical, showy ending that one could expect from early Prokofiev. This work gives a peaceful, sorrowful feel to the cycle. It beautifully complements the first piece in the set, creating a subtle arch to the form as a whole. Once again, dynamic markings vary only in the lowest range, from ppp to pp, and the unusual tempo indication (*Lento irrealmente*) indicates the touch and use of pedal necessary for this piece, similar to those of number seventeen. Unlike number seventeen, however, the use of a subtle *rubato* is encouraged.

## Scores consulted:

Prokofiev, Sergei. *Sarcasms, Visions fugitives, and Other Short Works for Piano.* ed. Dmitry Feofanov. Mineola, N.Y.: Dover, c. 2000.

Prokofiev, Sergei. *Visions fugitives: For Solo Piano,* Op. 22. Boca Raton, Fla.: Masters Music Publications, c. 1997.

Prokofiev, Sergei. *Visions fugitives: For Solo Piano,* Op. 22. New York: E.B. Marks, 1941.

Prokofiev, Sergei. *Visions fugitives,* Op. 22. ed. F. H. Schneider. London; New York: Édition russe de musique (S. et N. Koussewitzky): Boosey & Hawkes, c. 1922.

## Bibliography:

[1] Sergei Prokofiev, *Prokofiev by Prokofiev: A Composer's Memoir.* New York: Doubleday & Co., 1979, page 14.

[2] Ibid.

[3] Dorothea Redepenning, "Prokofiev, Sergey." In *Grove Music Online. Oxford Music Online,* http://ezproxy.missouriwestern.edu:2098/subscriber/article/grove/music/22402 (accessed September 3, 2009).

Phillips, Anthony, trans. and ed. *Sergey Prokofiev Diaries.* Ithaca, N.Y.: Cornell University Press, 2006.

Nice, D. *Prokofiev: from Russia to the West, 1891–1935.* New Haven: Yale University Press, c. 2003.

## Audio Credits:

Lance Miller, Recording Engineer
Alexandre Dossin, producer and pianist
Recorded at Beall Concert Hall,
University of Oregon School of Music and Dance

# VISIONS FUGITIVES

## Opus 22

# VISIONS FUGITIVES

Sergei Prokofiev
Op. 22

## 1.

Copyright © 2011 by G. Schirmer, Inc. (ASCAP) New York, NY
International Copyright Secured. All Rights Reserved.

*1917*

## 2.

**Andante** [♩ = 60–66]

Copyright © 2011 by G. Schirmer, Inc. (ASCAP) New York, NY
International Copyright Secured. All Rights Reserved.

*1916*

# 3.

**Allegretto** [♩ = 120–126]

Copyright © 2011 by G. Schirmer, Inc. (ASCAP) New York, NY
International Copyright Secured. All Rights Reserved.

*senza ped.*

*1916*

# 4.

Copyright © 2011 by G. Schirmer, Inc. (ASCAP) New York, NY
International Copyright Secured. All Rights Reserved.

1917

# 5.

**Molto giocoso** [♩ = 112–120]

Copyright © 2011 by G. Schirmer, Inc. (ASCAP) New York, NY
International Copyright Secured. All Rights Reserved.

*1915*

# 6.

**Con eleganza** [♩. = 126–132]

*p animato*

*senza ped.*

Copyright © 2011 by G. Schirmer, Inc. (ASCAP) New York, NY
International Copyright Secured. All Rights Reserved.

*1915*

# 7. (Harp)

**Pittoresco** [♩. = 40–44]

Copyright © 2011 by G. Schirmer, Inc. (ASCAP) New York, NY
International Copyright Secured. All Rights Reserved.

1916

# 8.

**Comodo [♩ = 92–96]**

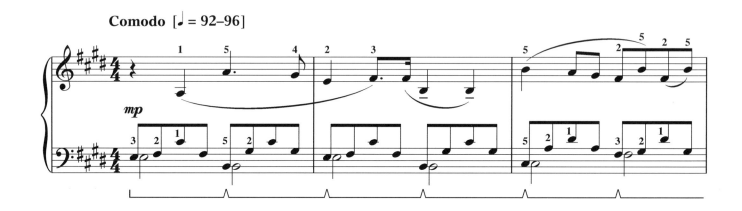

*mp*

*pp*

*legato, quasi senza ped.*

*pp*

*espress.*

*mp*

Copyright © 2011 by G. Schirmer, Inc. (ASCAP) New York, NY
International Copyright Secured. All Rights Reserved.

legato, quasi senza ped.

**Meno mosso**  [♩ = 72]

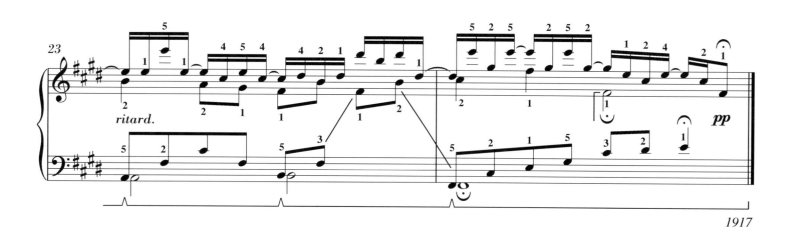

1917

# 9.

**Allegretto tranquillo** [♩ = 126]

Copyright © 2011 by G. Schirmer, Inc. (ASCAP) New York, NY
International Copyright Secured. All Rights Reserved.

1917

# 10.

**Ridiculosamente** [♩ = 92]

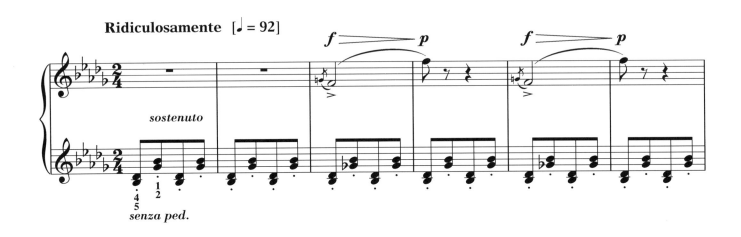

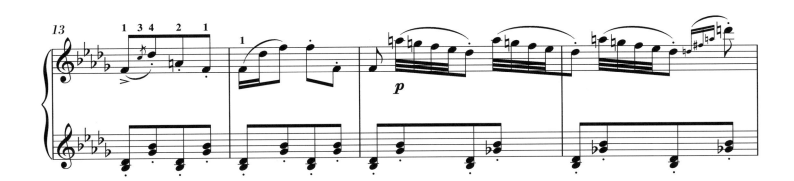

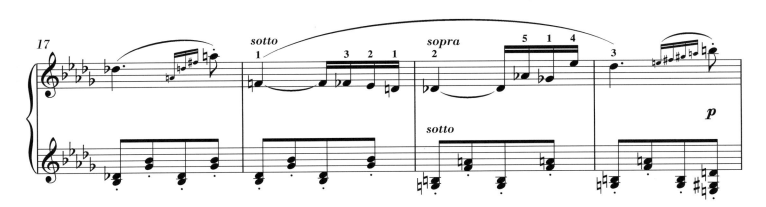

Copyright © 2011 by G. Schirmer, Inc. (ASCAP) New York, NY
International Copyright Secured. All Rights Reserved.

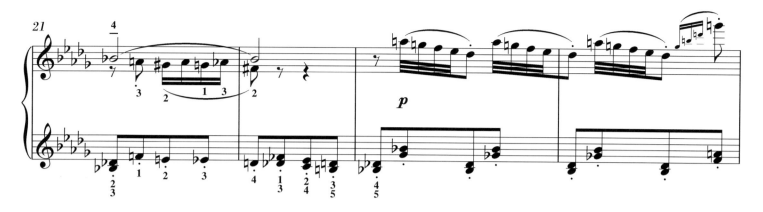

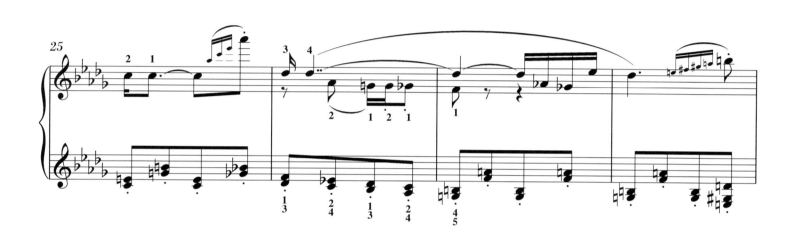

1915

# 11.

Copyright © 2011 by G. Schirmer, Inc. (ASCAP) New York, NY
International Copyright Secured. All Rights Reserved.

1917

# 12.

**Assai moderato**  [♩ = 76–80]

Copyright © 2011 by G. Schirmer, Inc. (ASCAP) New York, NY
International Copyright Secured. All Rights Reserved.

*1916*

# 13.

Allegretto [♩ = 76–80]

*1916*

Copyright © 2011 by G. Schirmer, Inc. (ASCAP) New York, NY
International Copyright Secured. All Rights Reserved.

# 14.

Copyright © 2011 by G. Schirmer, Inc. (ASCAP) New York, NY
International Copyright Secured. All Rights Reserved.

*D-F-C in some editions.

*1917*

34

# 15.

Inquieto [♩ = 144–152]

pp *una corda e senza ped.*

*Some editions have C-sharp here.

Copyright © 2011 by G. Schirmer, Inc. (ASCAP) New York, NY
International Copyright Secured. All Rights Reserved.

1917

# 16.

Copyright © 2011 by G. Schirmer, Inc. (ASCAP) New York, NY
International Copyright Secured. All Rights Reserved.

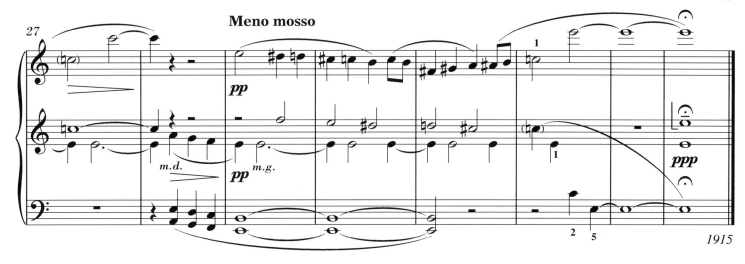

1915

## 17.

Copyright © 2011 by G. Schirmer, Inc. (ASCAP) New York, NY
International Copyright Secured. All Rights Reserved.

1915

# 18.

**Con una dolce lentezza** [♩ = 80–88]

Copyright © 2011 by G. Schirmer, Inc. (ASCAP) New York, NY
International Copyright Secured. All Rights Reserved.

*1917*

# 19.

**Presto agitatissimo e molto accentuato [♩ = 192–200]**

Copyright © 2011 by G. Schirmer, Inc. (ASCAP) New York, NY
International Copyright Secured. All Rights Reserved.

* Suggested performance:

1917

# 20.

**Lento irrealmente** [ ♩ (♩.) = 40–44]

Copyright © 2011 by G. Schirmer, Inc. (ASCAP) New York, NY
International Copyright Secured. All Rights Reserved.

1916

# ABOUT THE EDITOR

## ALEXANDRE DOSSIN

Considered by Martha Argerich an "extraordinary musician" and by international critics a "phenomenon" and "a master of contrasts," Alexandre Dossin keeps active performing, recording, and teaching careers.

Born in Brazil, where he lived until he was nineteen, Dossin spent nine years studying in Moscow, Russia, before establishing residency in the United States. This background allows him to be fluent in several languages and equally comfortable in a wide range of piano repertoire.

Currently on the faculty of the University of Oregon School of Music, Dossin is a graduate from the University of Texas-Austin and the Moscow Tchaikovsky Conservatory in Russia. He studied with and was an assistant of Sergei Dorensky at the Tchaikovsky Conservatory, and William Race and Gregory Allen at UT-Austin.

A prizewinner in several international piano competitions, Dossin received the First Prize and the Special Prize at the 2003 Martha Argerich International Piano Competition in Buenos Aires, Argentina. Other awards include the Silver Medal and Second Honorable Mention in the Maria Callas Grand Prix and Third Prize and Special Prize in the Mozart International Piano Competition.

He performed numerous live recitals for public radio in Texas, Wisconsin, and Illinois, including returning engagements at the Dame Myra Hess Memorial Concert Series. Dossin has performed in over twenty countries, including international festivals in Japan, Canada, the United States, Brazil, and Argentina, on some occasions sharing the stage with Martha Argerich. He was a soloist with the Brazilian Symphony, Buenos Aires Philharmonic, Mozarteum Symphony, and São Paulo Symphony, having collaborated with renowned conductors such as Charles Dutoit, Michael Gielen, Isaac Karabtchevsky, Keith Clark, and Eleazar de Carvalho.

Dossin has CDs released by Musicians Showcase Recording (2002), Blue Griffin (*A Touch of Brazil*, 2005), and Naxos (*Verdi-Liszt Paraphrases*, 2007; *Kabalevsky Complete Sonatas and Sonatinas*, 2009; *Kabalevsky Complete Preludes*, 2009; *Liszt in Russia*, 2011), praised in reviews by *Diapason*, *The Financial Times*, *Fanfare Magazine*, *American Record Guide*, *Clavier* and other international publications.

In the United States, Alexandre Dossin was featured as the main interview and on the cover of *Clavier* magazine and interviewed by *International Piano Magazine* (South Korea). He is an editor and recording artist for several Schirmer Performance Editions.

Dossin is a member of the Board of Directors for the American Liszt Society and the President of the Oregon Chapter of the American Liszt Society. He lives in the beautiful south hills of Eugene with his wife Maria, and children Sophia and Victor.

www.dossin.net